essential
Thai

essential

Thai

hamlyn

First published in 1994 by Chancellor Press

Reprinted in 1997, 1998, 2002 by
Hamlyn, a division of Octopus Publishing Group Limited
2-4 Heron Quays, London, E14 4JP

Designed and produced by SP Creative Design
Linden House, Kings Road, Bury St Edmunds, Suffolk, England
Editor and writer: Heather Thomas
Art Director: Al Rockall
Designer: Rolando Ugolini

ISBN 0 600 60587 6

A CIP catalogue record for this book is available from the
British Library

Printed in China

Acknowledgements
Special photography: James Murphy
Step-by-step photography: GGS Photographics, Norwich
Food preparation: Janet Smith and Dawn Stock
Styling: Jane McLeish

Notes

1. Standard spoon measurements are used in all recipes.
1 tablespoon = one 15ml spoon
1 teaspoon = one 5ml spoon

2. Both imperial and metric measurements have been
given in all recipes. Use one set of measurements
only and not a mixture of both.

3. Eggs should be medium unless otherwise stated.

4. Milk should be full fat unless otherwise stated.

5. Fresh herbs should be used unless otherwise stated.
If unavailable, use dried herbs as an alternative, but halve the
quantities stated.

6. Ovens should be preheated to the specified temperature.
If using a fan assisted oven, follow the manufacturer's
instructions for adjusting the time and the temperature.

CONTENTS

Introduction	6
Thai cooking ingredients	8
Soups and starters	10
Fish	28
Meat and poultry	46
Rice, noodles and eggs	68
Vegetables and salads	90
Desserts	102
Basic recipes	110
Index	112

INTRODUCTION

Thailand's hot and spicy dishes have a unique character of their own which distinguishes them from the cooking of the rest of Asia. Perhaps this is because Thailand is the only country in South-east Asia that has never been colonized, and thus its food and cookery, like its culture, have developed independently of outside influences. Meals are still prepared in the traditional way, and sharing food is an essential part of Thai family life and hospitality. In Thai homes, the food is always placed in the centre of the table, and everyone helps themselves from communal bowls.

Balance and harmony are very important, and several different dishes are served simultaneously to complement each other in colour, flavour and texture. There is an enormous variety of fresh food, and the ingredients are chosen carefully and then blended to create exquisite delicately flavoured crunchy salad(*yams*), fiery curries(*kangs*) and crisp stir-fries(*bhuds*) with noodles.

Thai food is characterized by its exuberant use of hot chillies, garlic, lemon grass, ginger and coconut, which are added to fresh seafood, meat, poultry and tropical vegetables and fruits and cooked in a myriad of ways.

Thai food takes quite a long time to prepare but the cooking methods are usually very simple and quick. You can prepare a meal in advance and then cook it literally in minutes, making it an extremely healthy fast food.

Aubergines

Thai aubergines are small and green with a crunchy texture. They are sometimes stuffed and deep fried, or may be eaten raw in salads.

Bamboo shoots

These are the tender young shoots of the bamboo plant. They are widely used in stir-fried dishes, and can be bought in cans in most supermarkets and specialist food stores and delicatessens.

Banana leaves

Some foods are baked or steamed in banana leaves, notably fish, dumplings and glutinous rice. If you cannot obtain fresh leaves, you can substitute oiled aluminium foil instead.

Bean curd

Made from puréed soya beans, bean curd is high in protein, low in fat and very nutritious. It has a soft texture and may be sliced or cubed. It can be purchased fresh or vacuum-packed from oriental stores, health food stores and some supermarkets.

Chillies

Thai chillies are small, narrow and tapering and may be red or green. In spite of their size – they are seldom more than two to three inches in length, and the tiny 'birdseye' chillies are no more than half an inch long – they are extremely hot and fiery, and great care should be taken when cutting them as the seeds can burn your skin. Always wash your hands immediately after handling chillies and avoid contact with the eyes. They can also be purchased dried.

The Thais love chillies, believing that they cool the body and stimulate the appetite, bringing balance and harmony to their food.

Coconut cream and milk

When added to spicy dishes and hot curries, coconut cream and milk create a distinctive creamy texture. You can make your own coconut milk by soaking fresh or desiccated coconut in water and then squeezing out the juice, or you can buy it ready-made. Coconut cream is the thick creamy liquid that forms on the surface of coconut milk when it is chilled in the refrigerator. You can skim it off to use in a variety of dishes. It is also available in cartons and cans. Remember that when you are cooking with coconut milk, you must take care that it does not curdle. When bringing it to the boil, stir it constantly, and never cover the wok or saucepan while it is cooking.

Coriander

The leaves and roots of this herb help to give Thai food its distinctive flavour. It resembles flat-leaf parsley in appearance, but here any similarity ends as it has a very intense, almost spicy flavour. In Thailand, coriander roots are usually

crushed with garlic and then used to flavour meat dishes and curries. The leaves are used universally to garnish every conceivable kind of savoury dish.

Curry pastes

These are traditionally made in a mortar by pounding together fresh herbs and hot spices, especially chillies, lemon grass, lime leaves, ginger, garlic and coriander. They may be red or green, depending on the colour of the chillies used. Western cooks can substitute a blender or electric grinder to make lighter work of the pounding.

Galanga

This mellow pine-flavoured root is the cousin of root ginger and a member of the ginger family. It is prepared in a similar fashion to fresh ginger: by peeling and crushing. It is often used in its powdered form – laos. A slice of fresh galanga is roughly equivalent to half a teaspoon of laos powder.

Ginger

Ginger is of Indian or Chinese origin but it is firmly established as an essential ingredient in Thai cookery. It is always used fresh rather than dried, and is peeled and then chopped or crushed before cooking. The ginger we buy in the West is often fibrous and quite dry in texture, but fresh ginger in Thailand is green and tender and highly flavoured.

Glutinous rice

Also known as 'sticky rice', this fragrant short-grain rice sticks together when cooked. It is used in both sweet and savoury dishes, and may also be ground into flour. It is usually cooked by steaming in banana leaves.

Lemon grass(takrai)

The aromatic bulbous root end of lemon grass looks rather like a small, slim leek and is used sliced, crushed or chopped in a wide range of Thai dishes, especially curries, soups and salads. The stem end is added whole to spicy soups and curries, and it yields a strong lemon fragrance and flavour. Ground to a fine powder, it is known as serai; one teaspoon of powder is equivalent to one blade of fresh lemon grass.

Lime leaves

Strongly citrus flavoured kaffir lime(makrut) leaves are used to flavour curries, soups and many other dishes. If you cannot obtain these, you could substitute bay leaves but the flavour will be different.

Nam pla(fish sauce)

This is the most commonly used flavouring in Thai food and is added to nearly all savoury dishes to accentuate the flavours of the other ingredients. It is made from salted anchovies and is quite salty and strongly flavoured. Bottled nam pla is now sold in most supermarkets.

Oyster sauce

This bottled sauce, which is made from oysters and soy sauce, is used to flavour stir-fried meat, poultry, fish and vegetable dishes.

Palm sugar

This heavy, strongly flavoured, hard brown sugar is made from the sap of the coconut palm tree. If you cannot obtain it, you can use dark brown Barbados sugar instead.

Soy sauce

Made from fermented soya beans, soy sauce may be light or dark and is quite salty. It is added to many chicken and stir-fried dishes, especially noodles.

Tamarind

This acidic tropical fruit resembles a bean pod and is usually sold dried or pulped. Dried tamarind should be soaked in warm water for at least 10 minutes before cooking. It is then squeezed to extract the pulp, which is sieved with the soaking water. The fibrous material is discarded, and the tamarind juice can be boiled and stored, or added immediately to many dishes.

Vermicelli

There are two types of vermicelli: rice sticks(sen mee) and transparent noodles(wun sen). Rice sticks are dried noodles made from rice flour. They come in a range of widths, ranging from quite wide ribbon noodles to very thin, string-like ones, and may be deep-fried or soaked in water and then boiled. Transparent noodles are made from mung bean flour and are always soaked in water before cooking.

Wonton wrappers

These squares of wafer-thin noodle dough are made from flour, eggs and water and can be bought fresh or frozen in a variety of sizes, although the most commonly used is 7cm/3 inches square. They are filled with delicious savoury mixtures and then steamed or fried.

Cooking utensils

Most meals are cooked in a wok, a wide rounded shallow pan with a curved base, which is perfect for deep frying, stir-frying and cooking curries and simmered dishes. The other most useful utensils are a large steamer(usually made of bamboo) and a granite mortar and pestle for grinding spices, pounding fresh herbs and making curry pastes. You need strong muscles to use this and you may prefer to opt for an electric blender or grinder, which takes all the hard work out of pounding. Sharp knives are essential for all the chopping and preparation, as is a cleaver for cutting up meat and poultry.

SHRIMP SOUP

Meng tom yam kung

750g/1½lb uncooked prawns

2 litres/3½ pints water

6 small kaffir lime leaves

1 tablespoon chopped lemon grass

2 teaspoons nam pla (fish sauce)

75ml/3 fl oz fresh lime juice

4 tablespoons sliced coriander leaves

3 tablespoons sliced spring onions

1 red chilli, seeded and sliced into
2.5cm/1 inch strips

salt and pepper

2 Pour the water into a large saucepan and bring to the boil. Add the lime leaves and chopped lemon grass, reduce the heat and simmer for 10 minutes. Add the nam pla and cook for a further 5 minutes.

3 Add the prawns and lime juice to the pan and cook gently over very low heat for a few minutes, until the prawns become firm and turn a pale pink colour.

1 Prepare the prawns: peel them and remove the dark vein running along the back. Wash them under running water, drain and pat dry with absorbent kitchen paper. Set aside while you make the soup.

4 Add the sliced coriander leaves, spring onions and red chilli strips to the soup. Check the seasoning, adding salt and pepper if wished, and serve very hot in small bowls.

PREPARATION: 5 MINUTES
COOKING: 25 MINUTES
SERVES: 6

CHICKEN AND COCONUT SOUP

Kai tom kah

2 Strain the stock into a clean saucepan. Add the coconut milk, stirring until blended. Bring to the boil and then simmer gently over low heat for 10 minutes.

3 Meanwhile, bone the chicken portions. Remove and discard the skin. Cut the chicken meat into very thin slices.

4 Stir the lime juice, sliced chicken and brown sugar into the soup. Simmer for 2–3 minutes, and then serve garnished with chillies and fresh basil leaves.

1 Bring the chicken stock, breast portions, onion, lemon grass, lime leaves and ginger to the boil. Cover the pan and simmer for 40 minutes.

1.2 litres/2 pints chicken stock
3 chicken breast portions
1 onion, finely chopped
3 stalks lemon grass, cut into 3 pieces and crushed
3 kaffir lime leaves
8 slices peeled root ginger
400ml/14 fl oz coconut milk
juice of 1 lime
2 teaspoons brown sugar
2 fresh red chillies, seeded and chopped
few basil leaves

PREPARATION: 15 MINUTES
COOKING: 1 HOUR
SERVES: 4–6

PRAWN AND SQUID HOT SOUP

Tom yum kung lae pla muk

1 Clean and wash the squid, and pat dry with absorbent kitchen paper. Cut off the tentacles and chop into small pieces. Cut the body into thin rings. Set aside while you make the soup.

3 Add the prepared prawns and squid to the pan and continue cooking gently over low heat for about 3–4 minutes until the prawns turn pink and firm. Add a little nam pla to taste.

250g/8oz squid
1.75 litres/2¾ pints chicken stock
6 kaffir lime leaves
1 stalk lemon grass, crushed
250g/8oz uncooked prawns, peeled and deveined
nam pla (fish sauce), to taste
4 fresh green chillies, sliced into rounds
2 garlic cloves, crushed
juice of 1 lime or lemon
salt and pepper
To garnish:
chopped coriander leaves

PREPARATION: 15 MINUTES
COOKING: 15 MINUTES
SERVES: 4

2 Pour the chicken stock into a large saucepan and bring to the boil. Add the lime leaves and lemon grass, then reduce the heat and simmer gently for about 5 minutes.

4 Stir the green chillies into the soup. Mix together the garlic with the lime or lemon juice in a small bowl until well blended, and then stir into the soup. Adjust the seasoning if necessary, adding salt and pepper to taste. Pour the soup into 4 warmed individual serving bowls. Serve sprinkled with chopped coriander.

FRIED WONTON

Geow grob

1 Put the minced pork in a small bowl with the chopped onion, garlic mixture and nam pla. Mix well together to combine all the ingredients to a thick paste.

3 Brush the edges of the wrappers with the egg yolk, and then fold the wrappers over to enclose the filling and make a triangular shape. Press the edges firmly together, sealing with more egg yolk if necessary.

2 Spread the wonton wrappers out on the work surface and put a teaspoon of the pork mixture in the centre of each wrapper.

| 250g/8oz minced pork |
| 1 tablespoon finely chopped onion |
| 2 teaspoons garlic mixture (see page 110) |
| 1/2 tablespoon nam pla (fish sauce) |
| 20 wonton wrappers (ones that are suitable for frying) |
| 1 egg yolk |
| oil for deep frying |
| **To serve:** |
| plum sauce or chilli sauce (see page 110) |

PREPARATION: 15 MINUTES
COOKING: 5-10 MINUTES
SERVES: 4-5

4 Heat the oil in a wok or large heavy based frying pan and fry the filled wonton, a few at a time, for about 5 minutes, until they are golden brown. Turn them over in the oil if necessary to brown both sides. Drain on absorbent kitchen paper and serve hot with plum sauce or chilli sauce.

PORK ON SKEWERS

Satay

500g/1lb pork fillet
1 teaspoon salt
2 teaspoons brown sugar
1 teaspoon ground turmeric
1 teaspoon ground coriander
1 teaspoon ground cumin
175ml/6 fl oz coconut milk
For the peanut sauce:
50g/2oz roasted peanuts
1 teaspoon salt
300ml/½ pint coconut milk
2 teaspoons red curry paste (see page 111)
2 tablespoons sugar
½ teaspoon lemon juice

2 Make the peanut sauce: grind the peanuts with the salt in a mortar until the mixture has the consistency of thick cream. Set aside.

3 Put half of the coconut milk in a saucepan with the curry paste. Heat gently for 3 minutes, stirring constantly. Stir in the creamed peanuts with the sugar, lemon juice and the remaining coconut milk. Simmer gently for 20–30 minutes, stirring occasionally to prevent it sticking to the pan. Transfer to a bowl.

4 Thread the marinated pork on to oiled bamboo skewers and cook on a barbecue or under a hot grill for 12–15 minutes, turning them several times and brushing frequently with the reserved coconut milk. Serve the kebabs with the peanut sauce.

1 Cut the pork into 5cm/2 inch long strips and place in a large bowl. Add the salt, sugar, turmeric, coriander, cumin and 4 tablespoons of the coconut milk. Mix thoroughly, using clean hands to knead the spices into the meat. Cover and leave to marinate for at least 2 hours.

PREPARATION: 5 MINUTES +
2 HOURS MARINATING
COOKING: 45 MINUTES
SERVES: 4

SPRING ROLLS

Poh piah tod

1 Make the filling: heat the oil in a wok or large deep frying pan. Add the garlic mixture and stir-fry for 1 minute until golden brown. Add the crabmeat, prawns and pork, and stir-fry for 10-12 minutes, or until lightly cooked. Add the vermicelli, mushrooms, nam pla, soy sauce, sugar and spring onions and stir-fry for 5 minutes until all the liquid has been absorbed. Set aside to cool.

3 Fold the sides over the filling and then roll up like a sausage. Brush the top edge with more beaten egg and then seal. Keep the filled rolls covered while you make the remaining spring rolls in the same way.

2 Separate the spring roll wrappers and spread them out under a clean tea towel to keep them soft. Put about 2 tablespoons of the filling on each spring roll wrapper, and brush the left and right borders with beaten egg.

1 x 250g/8oz package spring roll wrappers, each 13cm/5 inches square
1 egg, beaten
oil for deep frying
For the filling:
2 tablespoons vegetable oil
2 tablespoons garlic mixture (see page 110)
125g/4oz crabmeat
125g/4oz uncooked prawns, shelled and finely chopped
125g/4oz minced pork
125g/4oz vermicelli, soaked in boiling water until soft and cut into 1cm/½ inch lengths
125g/4oz mushrooms, chopped
2 tablespoons nam pla (fish sauce)
2 tablespoons light soy sauce
1 teaspoon sugar
5 spring onions, finely chopped

4 Heat the oil in a wok or deep-fat fryer and cook the spring rolls, a few at a time, for 5-8 minutes, or until golden brown. Turn them once during cooking so that they brown evenly. Drain on absorbent kitchen paper and serve them hot.

PREPARATION: 25 MINUTES
COOKING: 5-8 MINUTES
SERVES: 6

THAI DUMPLINGS

Kah nom jeeb

1 Put the pork, crabmeat, egg, water chestnuts, garlic mixture, nam pla, soy sauce and cornflour in a food processor or blender and process until well mixed, but not puréed. Alternatively, you can knead the ingredients by hand.

3 Bring up the edges all round into the centre to make a cup shape. Pinch the sides of the wonton 'cup' between your forefinger and thumb to form pleats. Shell the prawns, remove the veins and cut in half lengthways. Tuck half a prawn into each wonton dumpling.

2 Trim 1cm/½ inch off the 4 corners of each wonton wrapper to make an octagonal shape. Place a teaspoon of the pork filling mixture in the centre of each wrapper.

250g/8oz minced pork
250g/8oz crabmeat
1 egg
125g/4oz canned water chestnuts, drained
1 tablespoon garlic mixture (see page 110)
1 tablespoon nam pla (fish sauce)
1 tablespoon soy sauce
1 tablespoon cornflour
40 wonton wrappers (ones that are suitable for steaming)
20 uncooked prawns
oil for deep frying
To serve:
4 tablespoons soy sauce
4 tablespoons sweet and sour sauce
1 tablespoon garlic oil (see page 111)

PREPARATION: 25 MINUTES
COOKING: 15 MINUTES
SERVES: 8-10

4 Arrange the filled wontons in the top of one or two greased steamers and then steam gently for 15 minutes. Meanwhile, prepare the dipping sauce: mix the soy sauce and sweet and sour sauce together in a small bowl. Serve the hot dumplings, sprinkled with garlic oil, with the dipping sauce or some chilli sauce.

CHICKEN DUMPLINGS

Kha nom jeeb sai gai

3 tablespoons glutinous rice flour
275g/9oz rice flour
3 tablespoons arrowroot
350ml/12 fl oz water
2½ tablespoons vegetable oil
For the filling:
4 tablespoons vegetable oil
2 tablespoons garlic mixture (see page 110)
500g/1lb minced chicken
1 onion, finely chopped
3 tablespoons nam pla(fish sauce)
3 tablespoons sugar
To serve:
2 tablespoons garlic oil (see page 111)
½ cucumber, sliced
5 spring onions, sliced

2 Transfer the mixture to a large bowl and allow to cool slightly. When it is just warm, add the remaining arrowroot and knead the dough until it is smooth and shiny. Cover the bowl with a damp cloth while you make the filling.

3 Make the filling: heat 2 tablespoons of the oil in a wok and stir-fry the garlic mixture for 1 minute. Add the chicken and stir-fry for 4–5 minutes, until cooked. Stir in the onion, nam pla and sugar, and stir-fry until the liquid is absorbed. Transfer to a bowl and leave to cool.

1 Make the dough: put both the rice flours in a saucepan with 1 tablespoon of the arrowroot, and stir in the water and vegetable oil. Cook over moderate heat, stirring constantly, until the mixture forms a ball and leaves the sides of the pan clean.

PREPARATION: 30 MINUTES
COOKING: 10–15 MINUTES
SERVES: 6

4 Roll the dough into small balls, about 1cm/½ inch in diameter. Flatten each ball to a round and place 1 heaped teaspoon of filling in the centre of each. Draw up the sides to enclose the filling or fold over to form semi-circles, and crimp the edges. Line the top of a steamer with oiled foil or banana leaves, and arrange the dumplings on top. Steam over boiling water for 10–15 minutes. Serve brushed with garlic oil garnished with sliced cucumber and sliced spring onions.

FRIED GOLDEN BAGS
Tang tong

20 wonton wrappers

20 fresh chives, approx. 10cm/4 inches long

oil for deep frying

For the crabmeat filling:

75g/3oz canned water chestnuts, chopped

250g/8oz crabmeat

50g/2oz uncooked prawns, shelled and chopped

2 teaspoons garlic mixture (see page 110)

2 spring onions, chopped

1 fresh green chilli, seeded and chopped

1 tablespoon dark soy sauce

1 tablespoon nam pla (fish sauce)

To serve:

plum sauce or chilli sauce (see page 110)

1 Make the filling: put all the filling ingredients in a large mixing bowl and mix together until thoroughly combined. You should end up with a thick paste.

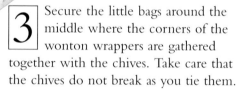

3 Secure the little bags around the middle where the corners of the wonton wrappers are gathered together with the chives. Take care that the chives do not break as you tie them.

2 Spread the wonton wrappers out on a flat surface and divide the crabmeat filling equally between them, putting a spoonful in the centre of each wrapper. Pull the 4 corners up into the middle to make little bags.

4 Heat the oil for deep frying in a wok or deep-fryer. Fry the little bags in batches, a few at a time, until they are crisp and golden brown. Remove and drain on absorbent kitchen paper. Serve very hot with either plum sauce or chilli sauce.

PREPARATION: 25 MINUTES
COOKING: 5-10 MINUTES
SERVES: 4-5

FRIED HOT FISH BALLS

Tod mun pla

1 Put the garlic, black peppercorns, coriander, sugar and dried red chillies in a food processor or blender and work to a smooth paste.

3 Shape the mixture into 20 small balls, about 2.5cm/1 inch in diameter. Heat the oil in a wok or deep frying pan and then fry the fish balls, a few at a time, until golden brown all over. Remove with a slotted spoon, drain and keep warm.

2 Add the fish fillets, a little at a time, and continue working to a smooth paste. Add the flour and soy sauce and process for a a few seconds. Transfer the mixture to a bowl.

4 garlic cloves, chopped
20 black peppercorns
4 stems coriander, finely chopped
pinch of sugar
3 large dried red chillies
750g/1½lb fish fillets, skinned
1 tablespoon plain flour
1 tablespoon soy sauce
5 tablespoons vegetable oil
For the salad:
½ cucumber, peeled and thinly sliced
1 teaspoon distilled vinegar
2 tablespoons water
1 teaspoon sugar
2 spring onions, finely chopped
1 small carrot, peeled and grated

4 Arrange the cucumber slices in a serving dish. Mix together the vinegar, water, sugar, spring onions and carrot, and sprinkle over the cucumber. Serve the cucumber salad with the fried hot fish balls.

PREPARATION: 15 MINUTES
COOKING: 5–10 MINUTES
SERVES: 4

29

PRAWN CURRY

Kaeng keao wan kung

1 Put the coconut milk in a jug and chill in the refrigerator for at least 1 hour, or until the thick milk rises to the surface. Scoop 250ml/8 fl oz off the top and put into a wok or heavy saucepan. Reserve the remaining coconut milk for later.

3 Shell and devein the prawns and wash them under running water. Pat dry and add to the mixture in the wok. Stir-fry for 3-4 minutes until they are firm and pink.

2 Bring the coconut milk to the boil and then simmer, uncovered, stirring occasionally, until the coconut oil begins to bubble to the surface and the liquid reduces to a quarter of its original volume. Add the curry paste and laos and bring to the boil. Cook over medium to high heat until most of the liquid evaporates.

4 Stir in the remaining coconut milk and nam pla and simmer for 6-8 minutes, stirring occasionally. Serve garnished with strips of green chilli and basil leaves.

| 750ml/1¼ pints coconut milk (see page 111) |
| 2 tablespoons green curry paste (see page 111) |
| 2 teaspoons ground laos |
| 750g/1½lb uncooked prawns |
| 2 tablespoons nam pla (fish sauce) |
| 1 tablespoon fresh green chilli, cut into 2.5cm/1 inch strips |
| 4 fresh basil leaves |

PREPARATION: 10 MINUTES + 1 HOUR CHILLING
COOKING: 30-35 MINUTES
SERVES: 4-6

CRAB IN THE SHELL

Bhou jah

4 crab shells, washed and dried

few fresh coriander leaves

2 fresh red chillies,
seeded and cut into strips

2 eggs

oil for deep frying

chilli sauce or nam pla (fish sauce) to serve

For the filling:

75g/3oz crabmeat

75g/3oz minced uncooked prawns

250g/8oz minced pork

1 egg

1 tablespoon garlic mixture (see page 110)

1 tablespoon nam pla (fish sauce)

1 tablespoon soy sauce

2 Pack the filling mixture into the crab shells and place them in the top of a steamer. Scatter with coriander leaves and strips of red chilli. Steam the filled crab shells over boiling water for 15 minutes, and then set aside to cool.

1 Prepare the filling: mix the crabmeat, prawns and pork in a small bowl. Stir in the egg, garlic mixture, nam pla and soy sauce, and mix well together.

3 Break the eggs into a shallow bowl and beat well. Dip the cooled crab shells, filled side down, into the egg mixture.

4 Heat the oil in a wok or deep-fat fryer, and fry the filled crab shells, one at a time, for 1-2 minutes or until the egg coating is golden. Remove with a slotted spoon and then drain on absorbent kitchen paper. Serve the crabs with chilli sauce or nam pla.

PREPARATION: 30 MINUTES
COOKING: 4-8 MINUTES
SERVES: 4

SOUR FISH CURRY

Kang som pla

350ml/12 fl oz water
500g/1lb cod fillet, sliced
2 tablespoons nam pla (fish sauce)
1 tablespoon sugar
2 tablespoons lemon juice
375g/12oz mixed vegetables, e.g. shredded cabbage, sliced courgettes, trimmed green beans and broccoli florets
For the kang som paste:
6 fresh or dried red chillies, seeded and sliced
2 teaspoons salt
1 tablespoon chopped mild onion
2 teaspoons shrimp paste

2 Bring the measured water to the boil in a medium-sized saucepan. Add half of the sliced cod fillet, then lower the heat and simmer gently for 5 minutes. Remove the fish with a slotted spoon.

3 Put the cooked fish in a food processor or blender together with the kang som paste. Blend the fish and paste until thick and smooth. Alternatively, pound the fish mixture in a mortar with a pestle.

1 Make the kang som paste: if using dried chillies, soak them in cold water for 10 minutes and then squeeze out as much liquid as possible. Put the chillies in a mortar with the salt and pound to a paste. Add the onion and shrimp paste and grind until smooth.

4 Transfer the puréed mixture to a clean saucepan and bring slowly to the boil. Stir in the nam pla, sugar and lemon juice. Add the vegetables and the remaining fish and stir well. Cover the pan and simmer for 10 minutes. Serve immediately.

PREPARATION: 20 MINUTES
COOKING: 25 MINUTES
SERVES: 4

SEAFOOD IN BATTER

Gung pla choob pang tod

| 1 | Combine the garlic mixture and nam pla in a shallow bowl. Peel and devein the prawns and cut the squid into rings (if using). Add to the dish and turn gently in the garlic marinade. Set aside for 5 minutes. |

| 2 teaspoons garlic mixture (see page 110) |
| 2 teaspoons nam pla (fish sauce) |
| 500g/1lb seafood, e.g. prawns and squid |
| oil for deep frying |

For the tempura batter:

| 1 egg |
| 150ml/¼ pint cold water |
| 125g/4oz self-raising flour |
| 2 tablespoons cornflour |
| 1 teaspoon baking powder |

To serve:

| shrimp dipping sauce (see page 110) |

PREPARATION: 25 MINUTES
COOKING: 5-10 MINUTES
SERVES: 4

| 2 | Make the tempura batter: lightly beat together the egg and water in a small bowl. Stir in the flour, cornflour and the baking powder. Do not over-mix; the batter should have a slightly lumpy texture. |

| 3 | Remove the prawns and squid from the garlic marinade and dip them quickly into the prepared tempura batter. Set aside while you heat the oil ready for frying. |

| 4 | Heat the oil for deep frying in a deep wok, a frying pan or a deep-fat fryer. When it is hot, fry the battered seafood, a few at a time, until puffed up and golden. Remove with a slotted spoon and drain on absorbent kitchen paper. Serve with shrimp dipping sauce. |

MUSSELS WITH THAI HERBS

Hoy mangpoo ob mor din

2.4 litres/4 pints fresh mussels

1.2 litres/2 pints water

6 kaffir lime leaves

rind of 1 lemon

2 blades lemon grass

1 tablespoon salt

3 fresh red chillies, sliced

3 spring onions, chopped

few coriander leaves, torn

1 Wash the mussels under running cold water and then scrape away any barnacles with a sharp knife. Remove the beards, and discard any mussels that are open.

2 Put the water in a large saucepan and bring to the boil. Add the kaffir lime leaves, lemon rind, lemon grass and salt. Add the mussels, cover the pan and bring back to the boil.

3 Cook the mussels, shaking the pan occasionally, until the mussels open. Drain them, reserving half of the cooking liquor. Transfer the mussels to a deep serving dish, discarding any that have not opened.

4 Strain the reserved stock, discarding the lime leaves, lemon rind and lemon grass. Bring to the boil, add the sliced red chillies and spring onions, and then boil vigorously for 2 minutes. Pour over the mussels and serve immediately.

PREPARATION: 20 MINUTES
COOKING: 20 MINUTES
SERVES: 4

PRAWNS IN COCONUT SAUCE

Gung penang

16 large uncooked prawns

2 tablespoons oil

1 large onion, finely chopped

2 stalks lemon grass, chopped

2 fresh red chillies, sliced

2.5cm/1 inch piece fresh ginger, shredded

1 tablespoon ground cumin

1 tablespoon ground coriander

2 tablespoons nam pla (fish sauce)

250ml/8 fl oz thick coconut milk

3 tablespoons roasted peanuts, coarsely ground

2 tomatoes, skinned and chopped

1 teaspoon sugar

juice of ½ lime

fresh coriander leaves, chopped

2 Heat the oil in a wok or heavy frying pan. Add the onion and fry until soft and golden. Add the chopped lemon grass, sliced red chillies, ginger, cumin and coriander, and sauté for 2 minutes.

3 Add the nam pla and coconut milk to the wok. Stir well and then add the peanuts and chopped tomatoes. Cook gently over low heat until the tomato is soft and the flavours of the sauce are well developed.

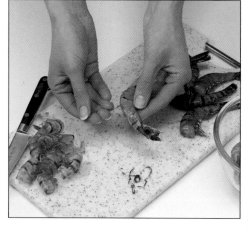

1 Remove the prawns from their shells, leaving the tails intact. Remove the dark veins running along the back of the prawns and then slit them down the underside from head to tail.

4 Stir in the prepared prawns and simmer gently for 5 minutes, or until the prawns are pink and tender. Add the sugar and transfer to a serving dish. Serve hot sprinkled with lime juice and chopped coriander leaves.

PREPARATION: 20 MINUTES
COOKING: 17–20 MINUTES
SERVES: 4

STEAMED FISH

Pla pah sah

1 large or 2 medium whole grey mullet or bass or grouper, scaled and cleaned

3 fresh red chillies, seeded and chopped

1.25cm/½ inch fresh root ginger, grated

3 spring onions, chopped

2 garlic cloves, crushed

1 stalk lemon grass, chopped

2 tablespoons nam pla (fish sauce)

For the stock:

40g/1½oz shredded cabbage

2 sticks celery, sliced

1 garlic clove, crushed

juice of 1 lime

250ml/8 fl oz fish stock or water

To serve:

chilli sauce (see page 110)

2 In a bowl, mix together the chopped red chillies, ginger, spring onions, garlic, lemon grass and nam pla. Spread this mixture over the fish.

1 Wash the fish under running cold water, inside and out. Pat dry with absorbent kitchen paper, and then slash the skin of the fish a few times with a sharp knife.

3 Place the fish on a rack or a perforated tray, and set above some boiling water in a large wok. Cover with the lid and steam for 15 minutes. Alternatively, use a large steamer or fish poacher.

4 Combine the cabbage, celery, garlic, lime juice and fish stock in a saucepan. Bring to the boil, and then pour over the fish in the wok. Continue steaming for 10 minutes, or until the fish is cooked and tender. Serve the steamed fish with the chilli sauce.

PREPARATION: 15 MINUTES
COOKING: 25 MINUTES
SERVES: 4

SPICY FISHCAKES
Tod mun pla

1 Put the chunks of cod fillet and red curry paste in a food processor or blender. Process until the fish is pounded to a paste. Alternatively, pound in a mortar with a pestle.

2 Transfer the fish mixture to a bowl and add the egg, nam pla and sufficient flour to knead with your hands into a stiff mixture. Work in the beans and lime leaves with your hands.

PREPARATION: 20 MINUTES
COOKING: 8-10 MINUTES
SERVES: 4-5

3 Form the fish mixture into 16-20 balls, and, using your hands, flatten each ball into a round, about 1cm/½ inch thick.

500g/1lb cod fillet, skinned and cut into chunks
3 tablespoons red curry paste (see page 111)
1 egg
3 tablespoons nam pla (fish sauce)
1-2 tablespoons rice flour
75g/3oz green beans, finely chopped
1 tablespoon finely shredded kaffir lime leaves
oil for deep frying
To serve:
chilli sauce (see page 110)

4 Heat the oil in a wok or large deep frying pan, and fry the fishcakes, a few at a time, for 4-5 minutes on each side, until they are cooked and golden. Take care not to overcook them. Drain on absorbent kitchen paper and serve hot with chilli sauce and a cucumber salad, if wished.

BEEF WITH CASHEW NUTS

Nauh bhud med ma maung

1 Heat ¹/₂ tablespoon of the sesame oil in a small frying pan, and fry the dried red chillies until crisp. Drain on absorbent kitchen paper to absorb the oil, and set aside while you stir-fry the beef and vegetables.

2 Heat the remaining sesame oil in a wok or a large frying pan. Add the garlic, onion and ginger and stir-fry quickly for about 3 minutes over high heat, until the onion is soft and golden brown.

PREPARATION: 10 MINUTES
COOKING: 10 MINUTES
SERVES: 4

3 tablespoons sesame oil
¹/₂ tablespoon chopped dried red chillies
1 garlic clove, finely chopped
1 onion, sliced
2.5cm/1 inch piece fresh root ginger, chopped
2–3 kaffir lime leaves, torn
500g/1lb lean beef, e.g. fillet, sirloin or rump steak, cut into strips
freshly ground black pepper
1 tablespoon soy sauce
1 teaspoon sugar
1 red pepper, seeded and sliced
1 green pepper, seeded and sliced
4 spring onions, sliced diagonally
125g/4oz roasted cashew nuts

3 Add the kaffir lime leaves and strips of beef, and stir-fry for 2–3 minutes. Season to taste with black pepper, and stir the soy sauce and sugar into the beef mixture.

4 Add the peppers and spring onions and stir-fry for 2–3 minutes. Add the reserved fried chillies and the roasted cashew nuts and quickly stir them through the mixture. Serve immediately with some boiled rice or fried noodles.

SWEET AND SOUR PORK

Bhud priew wharn

2 tablespoons vegetable oil

1 garlic clove, crushed

125g/4oz pork fillet

¹/₄ teaspoon freshly ground black pepper

1 tablespoon nam pla (fish sauce)

1 teaspoon sugar

¹/₂ cucumber

3 spring onions

1 tomato

1 fresh or canned pineapple ring, chopped

4 tablespoons chicken or vegetable stock

1 Heat the oil in a wok or deep frying pan. Add the crushed garlic and stir-fry quickly until it is golden, but not browned.

2 Slice the pork thinly and add to the wok, together with the freshly ground black pepper, nam pla and sugar. Stir-fry for 6-8 minutes, until the pork is cooked.

4 Add the vegetables to the wok with the chopped pineapple and the chicken or vegetable stock. Stir-fry for 3 minutes. Serve hot with plain boiled rice or noodles.

3 Prepare the vegetables: shred the cucumber and slice the spring onions across diagonally. Skin the tomato by plunging it into boiling water, and then roughly chop it.

PREPARATION: 10 MINUTES
COOKING: 11-13 MINUTES
SERVES: 4

SLICED PORK WITH HOT SAUCES

Moo thod katiem prik

375g/12oz pork fillet
1/2 teaspoon salt
1/4 teaspoon white pepper
2 tablespoons butter and oil, mixed
3 garlic cloves
1cm/1/2 inch piece fresh ginger, chopped
2 fresh red chillies, chopped
1 1/2 teaspoons ground cumin
For the chilli and ginger sauce:
2 fresh red chillies
2.5cm/1 inch piece fresh ginger, peeled
1/2 onion, grated
salt
For the tomato and chilli sauce:
2 tomatoes, skinned and chopped
2 garlic cloves, crushed
salt
pinch of sugar
1 teaspoon hot chilli powder

1 Slice the pork thinly, and rub with salt and pepper. Heat the butter and oil in a wok or small frying pan over moderate heat. Add the pork and stir-fry until lightly browned. Remove from the wok and keep warm.

3 Make the chilli and ginger sauce: put the chillies, ginger, onion and salt in a pestle and mortar. Pound the ingredients to a smooth, thick paste.

2 Chop the garlic finely and add to the wok with the ginger, chillies and cumin. Stir-fry for 2 minutes, and then return the pork to the wok. Stir-fry for 2 minutes over low heat, or until the meat is tender. If necessary, add a sprinkling of water to keep the meat moist.

4 Make the tomato and chilli sauce: put the chopped tomatoes and garlic in a small bowl, and mix in the salt, a good pinch of sugar and the hot chilli powder. Serve the stir-fried pork with the two hot sauces.

PREPARATION: 15 MINUTES
COOKING: 8-10 MINUTES
SERVES: 4

STUFFED THAI PANCAKE

Kai yud sai

3 tablespoons vegetable oil

1 garlic clove, crushed

125g/4oz minced pork

freshly ground black pepper

1 tablespoon nam pla (fish sauce)

½ tablespoon sugar

125g/4oz finely chopped onion

1 tomato, skinned and chopped

3 eggs, beaten

To garnish:

fresh coriander leaves

2 Stir-fry the pork and vegetable mixture in the wok for 5-10 minutes, until the pork is cooked and lightly browned, and the onion is tender and golden.

3 Heat the remaining oil in a clean wok or omelette pan, tilting it so that the oil coats the entire surface of the wok or pan. Pour away and discard any excess oil. Pour in the beaten eggs and swirl around the inside of the wok to form a thin skin.

1 Heat 2 tablespoons of the oil in a small wok or frying pan. Add the garlic and stir-fry quickly until golden brown. Add the minced pork, black pepper, nam pla, sugar, chopped onion and tomato.

4 Put the stir-fried vegetable and pork mixture in the centre of the omelette. Fold down the 4 sides to make a neat parcel. Slide out on to a warm serving dish, folded-side down, and serve garnished with coriander leaves.

PREPARATION: 10 MINUTES
COOKING: 12-17 MINUTES
SERVES: 2

MASAMAN CURRY

Kang masaman

1kg/2lb chuck steak

1.25 litres/2 pints water

200g/7oz creamed coconut, roughly chopped

150g/5oz roasted peanuts

nam pla (fish sauce) to taste

3 tablespoons tamarind water (see page 111)

coconut sugar to taste

For the curry paste:

1 teaspoon oil

7 dried chillies, seeded and finely chopped

1/2 teaspoon freshly ground black pepper

2 tablespoons coriander seeds

2 tablespoons cumin seeds

1 tablespoon shredded lemon grass

1 cinnamon stick

5 cardamom seeds

1/4 whole nutmeg, grated

1 teaspoon salt

1 onion, very finely chopped

5 garlic cloves, crushed

1/2 teaspoon dried shrimp paste

2 Make the curry paste: heat the oil in a pan and add the chillies, black pepper, coriander, cumin, lemon grass, cinnamon, cardamom and nutmeg. Cook over low heat, stirring constantly, until the mixture browns.

3 Transfer to a mortar or an electric blender or food processor, and work to a smooth paste. Add the salt, chopped onion, garlic and dried shrimp paste, and continue working the mixture until smooth.

4 Remove the cooked meat from the pan and keep warm. Add the creamed coconut to the liquid in the pan and heat gently, stirring. Add the peanuts and nam pla. Boil hard until the liquid is reduced by one-third. Add the curry paste and simmer for 5 minutes, stirring. Return the meat to the pan, cover and bring to the boil. Cook over medium heat for a few minutes. Add the tamarind water and coconut sugar. Serve hot.

1 Cut the steak into 2.5cm/1 inch squares, trimming off any excess fat. Put the steak and water in a large saucepan and bring to the boil. Lower the heat, cover the pan and simmer for about 1 hour, or until the meat is tender.

PREPARATION: 15 MINUTES
COOKING: 1 1/2 HOURS
SERVES: 6

BEEF IN OYSTER SAUCE

Nauh bhud num mun hoi hed

1 Put the oyster sauce, cornflour and freshly ground black pepper in a small shallow dish, and mix well together until the mixture is well blended and smooth.

2 Cut the fillet steak into thin slices. Add to the oyster sauce mixture and mix in gently until well coated. Set aside to marinate for at least 15 minutes before cooking.

3 Heat the oil in a wok or deep frying pan. Add the crushed garlic and stir-fry until golden. Add the marinated steak and continue stir-frying for 3-4 minutes until the meat is browned and medium-done.

| 2 tablespoons oyster sauce |
| 2 teaspoons cornflour |
| 1/2 teaspoon freshly ground black pepper |
| 250g/8oz fillet steak |
| 2 tablespoons vegetable oil |
| 1 garlic clove, crushed |
| 125g/4oz mushrooms, sliced |
| 6 spring onions, sliced diagonally |
| 125ml/4 fl oz chicken stock or water |

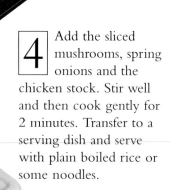

4 Add the sliced mushrooms, spring onions and the chicken stock. Stir well and then cook gently for 2 minutes. Transfer to a serving dish and serve with plain boiled rice or some noodles.

PREPARATION: 10 MINUTES +
15 MINUTES MARINATING
COOKING: 7-8 MINUTES
SERVES: 4

THICK RED BEEF CURRY
Kang panag nua

350g/12oz beef brisket, thinly sliced

1 tablespoon vegetable oil

2 tablespoons red curry paste (see page 111)

200ml/7 fl oz coconut milk (see page 111)

1 tablespoon nam pla (fish sauce)

1 tablespoon sugar

4 kaffir lime leaves

1-2 fresh green chillies

2 sprigs fresh basil

2 Heat the oil in a saucepan over moderate heat. Add the prepared red curry paste and stir-fry for 1 minute. Stir in 2 tablespoons of the coconut milk and cook, stirring constantly, for 5 minutes.

3 Add the cooked beef slices to the saucepan together with the nam pla, sugar, the remaining coconut milk and lime leaves. Bring to the boil, then lower the heat and simmer, stirring occasionally, for 15 minutes.

1 Place the beef in a medium-sized saucepan. Add sufficient water to cover and bring to the boil. Lower the heat and simmer for 1-1¼ hours, or until the meat is tender, skimming the liquid occasionally. Remove the beef slices with a slotted spoon and set aside.

4 Wearing rubber gloves if possible, slice the chillies into thin rounds and remove the seeds. Just before serving the curry, stir in the sliced chillies and the sprigs of basil.

PREPARATION: 5 MINUTES
COOKING: 1¼-1½ HOURS
SERVES: 2-3

FRIED PORK BALLS

Moo tod

1 Put the coriander stems, freshly ground black pepper, garlic and sugar in a mortar or blender, and then work to a smooth paste.

2 Put the pork and the coriander paste in a food processor or blender and add the nam pla. Process until the mixture is thick and smooth, and transfer to a bowl.

3 Form the mixture into about 20 small balls, approximately 2.5cm/ 1 inch in diameter. Roll the pork balls lightly in some flour.

4 Heat the oil in a wok or deep frying pan and add about 5 pork balls. Fry over moderate heat for 2-3 minutes, or until no liquid is released from the balls when pierced with a knife. Remove from the wok and keep warm while you fry the remaining balls. Serve hot garnished with fresh coriander leaves.

2 teaspoons chopped fresh coriander stems
2 teaspoons freshly ground black pepper
4 garlic cloves, peeled
pinch of sugar
500g/1lb minced pork
2 tablespoons nam pla (fish sauce)
flour for coating
4-5 tablespoons vegetable oil

To garnish:

fresh coriander leaves

PREPARATION: 15 MINUTES
COOKING: 12 MINUTES
SERVES: 4

CHICKEN CURRY
Kaeng phet kai

150g/5oz creamed coconut, roughly chopped

150ml/¼ pint water

4 large chicken breasts, boned, skinned and sliced

1 aubergine, peeled, cubed and blanched

2.5cm/1 inch piece fresh root ginger, chopped

few kaffir lime leaves, torn

For the curry paste:

½ teaspoon roasted coriander seeds

1 stalk lemon grass, finely chopped

grated rind of 1 lime

2 fresh green chillies, seeded and chopped

1 teaspoon cumin seeds

1 teaspoon shrimp paste

3 garlic cloves, crushed

1 small onion, finely chopped

To serve:

some fresh basil leaves

1 green chilli, cut into strips

3 Add the curry paste to the reserved coconut liquid and heat gently, stirring continuously. Continue stirring over low heat until the liquid starts to evaporate and thicken.

1 Put the creamed coconut and water in a large saucepan and heat gently, stirring all the time, until the coconut melts. Add the chicken and simmer for 10 minutes. Remove the chicken and keep warm. Reserve the coconut liquid.

PREPARATION: 10 MINUTES
COOKING: 30 MINUTES
SERVES: 4

2 Make the curry paste: grind all the ingredients together in a mortar with a pestle until you have a smooth paste. Alternatively, blend them at high speed in a food processor or blender until smooth.

4 Add the reserved chicken, cubed aubergine, ginger and kaffir lime leaves, and cook gently for a few minutes. Serve the curry sprinkled with basil leaves and green chillies, with noodles or boiled rice.

STUFFED CHICKEN WINGS

Peag gai sord sai

1 Prepare the chicken: remove the top part of each wing. Your aim is to bone the wings without damaging the skin. Cut around the bones with a small sharp knife and ease them out. Alternatively, break the wing joint and work the bones loose with your fingers. Turn the wings inside out to remove the bones.

2 Make the filling: put the chicken and vermicelli in a bowl with the chopped water chestnuts, garlic mixture, beaten egg, nam pla and soy sauce. Mix until the ingredients are thoroughly combined.

PREPARATION: 30 MINUTES
COOKING: 23-24 MINUTES
SERVES: 4

3 Carefully stuff each boned chicken wing with the stuffing mixture. Place in the top of 1 large or 2 small steamers, and steam over boiling water for 20 minutes. Remove and cool.

16 chicken wings
300g/11oz minced chicken
125g/4oz vermicelli, softened in boiling water and cut in 1cm/¹/₂ inch lengths
125g/4oz drained canned water chestnuts, finely chopped
1 tablespoon garlic mixture (see page 110)
1 egg, lightly beaten
2 tablespoons nam pla(fish sauce)
2 tablespoons soy sauce
For stir-frying:
1 tablespoon oil
2 tablespoons garlic mixture (see page 110)
2 tablespoons nam pla (fish sauce)
chilli sauce to serve (see page 110)

4 Heat the oil for stir-frying in a wok or large frying pan. Add the garlic mixture and nam pla, and then add the chicken wings. Stir-fry briskly for 3-4 minutes until golden. Serve with chilli sauce.

GINGER CHICKEN WITH HONEY

Pad king kai

5 spring onions

50g/2oz fresh ginger

2 tablespoons vegetable oil

3 chicken breasts, skinned and boned

3 chicken livers, chopped

1 onion, sliced

3 garlic cloves, crushed

2 tablespoons dried Chinese black mushrooms, soaked in warm water for 20 minutes

2 tablespoons soy sauce

1 tablespoon honey

2 Heat the oil in a wok or a large heavy-based frying pan. Cut the chicken into small pieces and add to the wok with the chicken livers. Fry for 5 minutes, then remove with a slotted spoon and set aside.

3 Add the onion to the wok and fry gently until soft. Add the garlic and the drained mushrooms and stir-fry for 1 minute. Return the cooked chicken pieces and chicken livers to the wok.

1 Cut the spring onions into 1cm/½ inch pieces. Put in a bowl, cover with cold water and leave to soak until required. Chop the ginger finely, mix with a little cold water, then drain and squeeze to remove its hotness. Rinse under cold running water and drain well.

4 Mix the soy sauce and honey, stirring until blended. Pour over the chicken and stir well. Add the drained ginger and stir-fry for 2-3 minutes. Add the drained spring onions, and transfer to a serving dish. This dish tastes even better if it is cooked the day before and then reheated.

PREPARATION: 15 MINUTES
COOKING: 15 MINUTES
SERVES: 4

RICE VERMICELLI WITH SAUCE

Pad mee krob

1 Heat the oil for deep frying in a heavy saucepan or deep-fat fryer to 190°C/375°F. Fry the rice vermicelli in small batches for about 30 seconds, until the strands swell and float. Drain and set aside. Take care that you fry only a little at a time as it expands a lot and could overflow the pan.

3 Now add the peeled prawns and crabmeat and cook for 2-3 minutes, until the prawns firm up and turn pink. Stir in the brown sugar, tamarind water, salt and soy sauce.

2 Make the sauce: heat the oil in a wok or deep frying pan. Add the onion and garlic and fry for a few minutes, until lightly brown.

| vegetable oil for deep frying |
| 50g/2oz rice vermicelli, broken into pieces |

| **For the sauce:** |
| 1 tablespoon vegetable oil |
| 1 onion, finely chopped |
| 2 garlic cloves, crushed |
| 250g/8oz uncooked prawns, peeled |
| 75g/3oz crabmeat |
| 2 teaspoons brown sugar |
| 2 tablespoons tamarind water (see page 111) |
| 1 teaspoon salt |
| 1 tablespoon soy sauce |

| **To garnish:** |
| 2 teaspoons finely grated orange rind |
| 2 red chillies, shredded |
| chopped coriander leaves |
| 125g/4oz fresh bean sprouts |

4 Add the fried vermicelli and stir well. Adjust the seasoning if necessary, and then heat through gently. Transfer to a warm serving dish and garnish with orange rind, chillies and coriander. Arrange the bean sprouts around the edge of the dish. Serve hot.

PREPARATION: 15 MINUTES
COOKING: 10 MINUTES
SERVES: 4

RICE VERMICELLI IN COCONUT MILK

Meeh ka ti

1 Bring a large saucepan of water to the boil, add the soaked rice vermicelli and cook, stirring occasionally, for 15 minutes. Drain the vermicelli well and set aside.

3 In a large wok or saucepan, bring the coconut milk to the boil. Cook over high heat for 10 minutes, until a film of oil forms on top. Stir in the onion, prawns, soya bean flavouring, sugar and tamarind or lemon juice. Cook for 5 minutes, and then transfer half of the mixture to a bowl and keep warm.

2 Heat the oil in an omelette pan or small frying pan and add the eggs. Tilt the pan to form an omelette, lifting the sides of the omelette to allow any uncooked egg mixture to flow underneath. Remove the cooked, set omelette from the pan and slice into thin shreds. Keep warm.

PREPARATION: 15 MINUTES + SOAKING TIME
COOKING: 45 MINUTES
SERVES: 4

250g/8oz soaked rice vermicelli
2 teaspoons oil
2 eggs, beaten
500ml/18 fl oz coconut milk (see page 111)
½ onion, roughly chopped
250g/8oz uncooked prawns, shelled
4 tablespoons salted soya bean flavouring
2 tablespoons sugar
2 tablespoons tamarind juice or 1 tablespoon lemon juice
300g/11oz bean sprouts
125g/4oz spring onions, chopped

To garnish:

3 tablespoons chopped coriander leaves
2 red chillies, seeded and sliced
1 lemon, sliced lengthways

4 Add the reserved vermicelli to the mixture in the wok. Mix well and cook for 5 minutes. Stir in half of the bean sprouts and spring onions. Pile the vermicelli mixture on to a serving dish and top with the reserved prawn mixture and shredded omelette. Garnish with coriander, chillies and lemon slices, and serve with the remaining bean sprouts and spring onions.

CRISPY RICE WITH DIPPING SAUCE

Khow tung nah tung

250g/8oz glutinous rice
oil for deep frying

For the sauce:

125ml/4 fl oz coconut milk
50g/2oz minced pork
50g/2oz minced prawns
1 teaspoon garlic mixture (see page 110)
1½ tablespoons nam pla
1½ tablespoons sugar
50g/2oz finely chopped onion
50g/2oz ground roasted peanuts

To garnish:

coriander leaves
crisply fried strips of red chilli

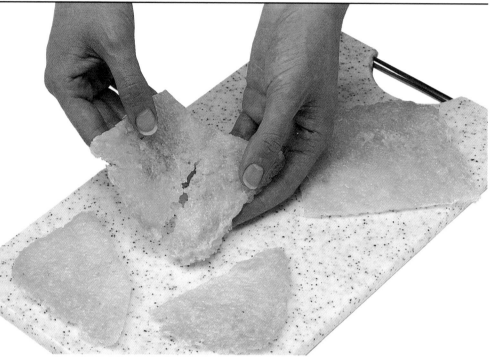

1 Put the rice in a saucepan, cover with water and boil until the rice is sticky and thoroughly cooked. Drain through a sieve and spread it out in a very thin layer on some greased baking trays. Press down well and leave to dry in a warm place or a cool oven (120°C/250°F/Gas Mark ½). This drying process takes several hours.

PREPARATION: 20 MINUTES + DRYING TIME
COOKING: 35 MINUTES
SERVES: 4

2 When completely dry and firm, remove the rice from the baking trays with a spatula or fish slice and then break into large pieces.

3 Heat the oil until it is very hot and then drop in some of the rice pieces. Deep fry quickly until golden. Remove from the oil and drain on absorbent kitchen paper. Cook the remaining rice in the same way.

4 Bring the coconut milk to the boil in a saucepan. Stir in the pork and prawns, and add the garlic mixture, nam pla, sugar, onion and peanuts. Mix well, reduce the heat and simmer for 20 minutes, stirring occasionally. Pour into a serving dish and garnish with coriander and chilli strips. Serve as a dip with the crispy rice.

FRIED RICE WITH PORK

Khow bhud mhoo

1 Crush the garlic in a pestle and mortar, or use a garlic crush. Heat the oil in a wok or a large deep frying pan. Add the garlic and stir-fry for 1 minute until golden brown.

3 Break the eggs into the wok or frying pan, and cook for 2 minutes, stirring vigorously. Add the tomato paste, sugar, the remaining soy sauce and the sliced onion. Stir-fry briskly for 1 minute.

4 Add the rice and continue stir-frying for 5 minutes. Transfer the mixture to a shallow serving dish or 4 serving plates and garnish with the sliced cucumber, lemon wedges, coriander leaves and shredded red chilli. Serve immediately.

2 Add the slices of pork fillet to the wok together with 1 teaspoon of the light soy sauce and then stir-fry for 5 minutes over medium heat.

1 garlic clove
2 tablespoons vegetable oil
150g/5oz pork fillet, sliced
3 tablespoons light soy sauce
2 eggs
1 tablespoon tomato paste
1 tablespoon sugar
1 small onion, sliced
750g/1¹/₂lb cooked rice (about 175g/6oz raw weight)

To garnish:

¹/₄ cucumber, thinly sliced
1 lemon, cut in wedges
2 tablespoons chopped coriander leaves
1 red chilli, seeded and shredded

PREPARATION: 10-15 MINUTES
COOKING: 15 MINUTES
SERVES: 4

THAI-STYLE FRIED RICE STICKS
Geuy teuw bhud Thai

1 Put the rice sticks in a large bowl and cover with cold water. Leave them to soak for at least 2 hours, or until they are soft. Drain the rice sticks well and set aside.

3 Add the dried shrimp, preserved turnip, ground chilli and the crushed peanuts, stirring all the time until well mixed.

2 Heat the oil in a wok or a large deep frying pan. Add the garlic and stir-fry for 1 minute, until golden. Add the chicken, crabmeat and prawns, and stir-fry for 3 minutes. Stir in the drained rice sticks, nam pla, sugar, lemon juice and pepper, and cook for 1 minute.

PREPARATION: 15 MINUTES +
2 HOURS SOAKING
COOKING: 10 MINUTES
SERVES: 4

125g/4oz rice sticks
2 tablespoons vegetable oil
1 garlic clove, crushed
125g/4oz chicken breast, thinly sliced
125g/4oz crabmeat
125g/4oz uncooked prawns, shelled and deveined
2 tablespoons nam pla (fish sauce)
2 tablespoons sugar
1/2 tablespoon lemon juice
1/4 teaspoon freshly ground black pepper
1 tablespoon ground dried shrimp
1 tablespoon chopped preserved turnip
1/2 teaspoon ground chilli
2 tablespoons crushed roasted peanuts
1 egg
2 tablespoons chopped spring onion tops
125g/4oz bean sprouts

To serve:

1 lemon, sliced and quartered
50g/2oz fresh bean sprouts

4 Break the egg into the wok and continue stirring. Add the spring onion tops and bean sprouts, and then stir-fry for 3 more minutes until the egg is set and the rice sticks are tender. If the rice sticks are hard, add 2 more tablespoons of water and cook until absorbed. Serve garnished with sliced lemon and bean sprouts.

RICE STICKS WITH BEEF SAUCE

Geuy teuw nah sub

1 Spread out the soaked rice sticks in a large shallow dish. Sprinkle the rice sticks with dark soy sauce and mix thoroughly, using 2 spoons or chopsticks. Make sure that all the rice sticks are coated in soy sauce.

2 Heat 2 tablespoons of the vegetable oil in a wok or a deep frying pan and add the rice sticks. Stir-fry for 3-5 minutes, then transfer to a serving dish and keep warm.

PREPARATION: 10 MINUTES +
2 HOURS SOAKING
COOKING: 25 MINUTES
SERVES: 4-6

3 Heat the remaining oil in the wok, add the garlic and stir-fry for 1 minute or until golden brown. Add the beef, nam pla, curry powder, sugar and black pepper and stir well.

500g/1lb soaked rice sticks
2 tablespoons dark soy sauce
4 tablespoons vegetable oil
1 garlic clove, crushed
300g/10oz minced beef
$1/2$ tablespoon nam pla (fish sauce)
$1/2$ tablespoon curry powder
1 teaspoon sugar
$1/4$ teaspoon freshly ground black pepper
1 tablespoon cornflour
3 tablespoons light soy sauce
1 small onion, chopped
1 tomato, chopped
350ml/12 fl oz chicken stock
To serve:
1 lettuce, separated into leaves
2 tablespoons chopped coriander leaves

4 In a bowl, mix the cornflour to a paste with the light soy sauce. Stir into the beef mixture and cook for 10-15 minutes, stirring frequently, until the beef is cooked and crumbly. Stir in the onion, tomato and stock and bring to the boil. Lower the heat and simmer for 5 minutes. Serve the rice sticks on a bed of lettuce topped with the beef mixture. Garnish with coriander.

SPICY FRIED RICE

Khow bhud khie mau

| 125g/4oz minced beef |
| 1 x 220g/8oz can red kidney beans, drained |
| 1½ tablespoons nam pla (fish sauce) |
| 1 tablespoon dark soy sauce |
| 4 red chillies, seeded and finely chopped |
| 3 garlic cloves, crushed |
| ½ teaspoon salt |
| 2 tablespoons vegetable oil |
| 10 green beans, trimmed and cut in 1.25cm/ ½ inch lengths |
| 750g/1½lb boiled long-grain rice (about 175g/6oz raw weight) |
| 1 tablespoon sugar |
| salt and freshly ground black pepper |
| 4 tablespoons roughly chopped fresh basil leaves |

1 Put the minced beef and drained kidney beans in a bowl. Mix well and then stir in the nam pla and soy sauce. Cover the bowl and set aside for 30 minutes to allow the different flavours to blend.

3 Add the beef and kidney bean mixture to the wok, and cook, stirring constantly, for 3 minutes, or until the beef is lightly browned. Add the green beans and stir-fry for 3 more minutes over moderate heat.

4 Stir in the cooked rice and sugar, and cook, stirring, until the rice is hot and all the ingredients are thoroughly mixed. Add salt and pepper or more nam pla to taste if necessary. Mix in the basil leaves and transfer to a serving dish.

2 Mix the chopped chillies, garlic and salt together in another bowl. Heat the oil in a wok or large frying pan and then add the chilli mixture. Stir-fry briskly for 1 minute.

PREPARATION: 10 MINUTES +
30 MINUTES MARINATING
COOKING: 10 MINUTES
SERVES: 4

FRIED NOODLES WITH VEGETABLES

Geuy teuw rard nah

1 Heat half of the oil in a wok or large deep frying pan. Add half the garlic and stir-fry for 1 minute until golden brown. Add the noodles and soy sauce and cook, stirring constantly, for 3-5 minutes. Transfer to a serving dish and keep warm.

3 Add the shredded cabbage and broccoli florets to the meat mixture in the wok, and stir-fry for 3 more minutes.

4 tablespoons vegetable oil
2 garlic cloves, crushed
125g/4oz medium-sized egg noodles
2 teaspoons dark soy sauce
125g/4oz mixed sliced chicken breast, prepared squid and shelled prawns
1/2 teaspoon freshly ground black pepper
2 tablespoons nam pla (fish sauce)
125g/4oz mixed shredded cabbage and broccoli florets
300ml/1/2 pint chicken stock
1 tablespoon cornflour
1 tablespoon salted soya bean flavouring
2 tablespoons sugar

2 Heat the remaining oil in the wok and add the rest of the garlic. Stir-fry for 1 minute until golden brown. Add the chicken breast, squid, prawns, ground black pepper and nam pla. Stir-fry for 5 minutes.

PREPARATION: 10 MINUTES
COOKING: 20 MINUTES
SERVES: 4

4 Stir in the chicken stock. Mix the cornflour with 2 tablespoons of water and stir into the wok. Add the soya bean flavouring and sugar, and bring to the boil. Lower the heat and cook for 3 minutes, stirring constantly. Pour the thickened sauce over the noodles and serve immediately.

EGG-FRIED NOODLES

Gung ob moh din

4 tablespoons groundnut oil

1 garlic clove, crushed

1 shallot or small onion, thinly sliced

125g/4oz egg noodles

grated rind of 1 lime

2 teaspoons soy sauce

2 tablespoons lime juice

125g/4oz sliced chicken breast or
pork fillet

125g/4oz crabmeat or squid

125g/4oz shelled prawns

freshly ground black pepper

1 tablespoon yellow soya bean paste

1 tablespoon nam pla (fish sauce)

2 tablespoons brown sugar

2 eggs

2 fresh red chillies, seeded and chopped

few coriander leaves, chopped

2 Plunge the egg noodles into boiling water for a few seconds. Drain well and then add to the wok. Stir-fry with the grated lime rind, soy sauce and lime juice for 3-4 minutes. Remove, drain and keep warm.

3 Add the remaining oil to the wok together with the chicken, crabmeat and prawns. Stir-fry over high heat until cooked. Season with ground black pepper, and stir in the soya bean paste, nam pla and sugar.

1 Heat half of the oil in a wok or heavy frying pan. Add the garlic and the shallot, and then stir-fry quickly until golden and tender.

4 Break the eggs into the wok and stir gently until the mixture sets. Add the chillies and check the seasoning. Mix in the noodles and heat through over low heat. Serve garnished with chopped coriander.

PREPARATION: 10 MINUTES
COOKING: 20 MINUTES
SERVES: 4

CRISPY RICE VERMICELLI
Meeh grob

oil for deep frying

150g/5oz rice vermicelli

6 tablespoons vegetable oil

1 egg, beaten

1 tablespoon sliced shallots

1 tablespoon sliced garlic

50g/2oz uncooked prawns, shelled and cut in half lengthways

50g/2oz chicken breast, thinly sliced

2 tablespoons tamarind water

4 tablespoons brown sugar

1 tablespoon salted soya bean flavouring

1 tablespoon nam pla (fish sauce)

To garnish:

1 fresh red chilli, seeded and sliced

2 tablespoons chopped coriander leaves

1 Heat the oil in a wok or deep-fat fryer until the temperature reaches 190°C/375°F. It will be ready when a piece of vermicelli, dropped into the wok, pops open immediately. Deep fry the vermicelli in batches until it pops and turns a rich creamy colour. Remove, drain on absorbent kitchen paper and keep warm without covering, or it will become soft.

PREPARATION: 15 MINUTES
COOKING: 17–18 MINUTES
SERVES: 4

2 Heat a little of the vegetable oil in a small pan and add the beaten egg, tilting the pan until it covers the base. Remove the omelette when it is set and cooked, and roll up and cut into thin strips. Keep them warm.

3 Heat the remaining oil in a wok and stir-fry the shallots and garlic until tender and golden brown. Remove, drain and keep warm. Add the prawns and sliced chicken breast to the wok and stir-fry for 5 minutes. Drain off any excess oil.

4 Stir in the tamarind juice, sugar, soya bean flavouring and nam pla. Cook for 5 minutes until sticky. Add the vermicelli, shallots and garlic to the pan, mix well and cook over very low heat for 2–3 minutes. Transfer to a serving dish, top with the omelette strips, and serve garnished with sliced chilli and coriander leaves.

THAI HARD-BOILED EGGS

Khai loog kheoy

1 Bring a saucepan of water to the boil. Stir in the vinegar, then lower the heat and carefully add the eggs. Boil gently for 6-7 minutes, then drain and run the eggs under cold water until cool. Shell them carefully and set aside.

3 Heat the remaining oil in a wok or large frying pan. Add the eggs and fry, turning constantly with a wooden spoon, until golden brown. Remove each egg as it browns and drain on absorbent kitchen paper.

2 Heat ½ tablespoon of the oil in a small wok or frying pan. Add the dried red chillies and fry until they are crisp. Drain on absorbent kitchen paper and set aside.

PREPARATION: 15 MINUTES
COOKING: 15 MINUTES
SERVES: 4-6

1 teaspoon vinegar
6 eggs
4½ tablespoons vegetable oil
1 tablespoon dried red chillies
4 red shallots, finely chopped
120ml/4 fl oz tamarind sauce
2 teaspoons dark soy sauce

4 Add the shallots to the wok and fry quickly until golden brown. Transfer to a small dish and keep warm. Pour away all but 2 tablespoons of oil from the wok. Add the tamarind sauce and soy sauce, and boil until the mixture thickens. Meanwhile, quarter the eggs lengthways and arrange on a serving dish. Pour the tamarind sauce over the top and sprinkle with the fried shallots and chillies.

NORTH-EASTERN BEEF SALAD

Nua nam tok

2 tablespoons glutinous rice

300g/11oz rump steak

4 tablespoons water

2 onions, finely chopped

3 tablespoons fresh mint leaves, chopped

1 teaspoon ground chilli

2 tablespoons lemon juice

2 tablespoons nam pla (fish sauce)

1/2 teaspoon sugar

For the garnish:

1 lettuce, separated into leaves

2 tablespoons chopped fresh coriander

2 Put the steak on a rack in a grill pan and cook under a preheated grill for about 2 minutes on each side. Reduce the heat and cook for a further 4 minutes. Set aside to cool.

3 Slice the grilled steak thinly and put in a saucepan with the water Cook over high heat for about 1 minute, stirring constantly.

1 Put the glutinous rice in a saucepan over moderate heat and dry-fry, stirring constantly, for 10 minutes, or until the grains are light brown in colour. Remove from the heat and grind in a food processor or pound in a mortar with a pestle until fine.

4 Remove the saucepan from the heat and stir in the ground rice, onions, mint, chilli, lemon juice, nam pla and sugar. Arrange the mixture on a bed of lettuce leaves in a shallow serving dish. Scatter the chopped coriander over the top and serve immediately.

PREPARATION: 20 MINUTES
COOKING: 7 MINUTES
SERVES: 4

91

CHICKEN SALAD

Yam kai

4 boned chicken breasts

garlic oil for brushing (see page 111)

some crisp lettuce leaves

5 spring onions, chopped

½ cucumber, peeled and diced

125g/4oz oyster mushrooms,
thinly sliced

125g/4oz canned water chestnuts,
drained and sliced

For the dressing:

3 tablespoons nam pla(fish sauce)

juice of 2 limes

1 garlic clove, crushed

2 teaspoons soft brown sugar

2 fresh red chillies, seeded and
cut into shreds

To garnish:

1 tablespoon chopped fresh coriander

sliced red and green chillies

2 Arrange the lettuce leaves in a serving dish, and sprinkle with the chopped spring onions, diced cucumber, sliced oyster mushrooms and water chestnuts.

1 Preheat the grill. Place the chicken breasts on a grill pan and brush liberally with garlic oil. Grill until cooked right through and golden brown, turning once during cooking to brown both sides. Set aside to cool while you prepare the salad.

PREPARATION: 15 MINUTES
COOKING: 20 MINUTES
SERVES: 4

3 Make the dressing: put the nam pla, lime juice, garlic, sugar and shredded red chillies in a small saucepan. Place the pan over low heat and cook very gently, stirring all the time until the sugar has dissolved. Remove from the heat.

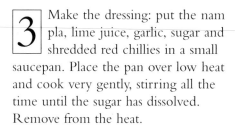

4 Cut the cooked chicken into strips and arrange them on top of the salad. Cover with the warm dressing, and then garnish with chopped coriander and sliced red and green chillies. Serve the salad warm.

CURRIED VEGETABLE SALAD

Nam prik deng Thai

2 sticks celery

4 carrots

125g/4oz cabbage

125g/4oz thin green beans

½ red pepper

½ green pepper

250g/8oz bean sprouts

227g/7½oz can water chestnuts, drained and sliced

For the curry dressing:

125g/4oz creamed coconut

150ml/¼ pint water

2 tablespoons groundnut oil

2 tablespoons red curry paste (see page 111)

2 tablespoons dark soy sauce

juice of 1 lime

2 teaspoons brown sugar

¼ teaspoon salt

1 teaspoon ground coriander

2 teaspoons ground cumin

3 tablespoons chopped roasted peanuts

To garnish:

few sprigs of fresh mint

2 Bring a large saucepan of water to the boil, and plunge in the prepared vegetables. Blanch them by boiling for 3-4 minutes. They should retain their fresh colour and be slightly tender but still crisp. Drain and mix in a bowl with the bean sprouts and water chestnuts.

3 Make the curry dressing: put the creamed coconut in a bowl and cover with the water. Stir well until the coconut cream has completely dissolved, and set aside.

1 Prepare the vegetables: roughly chop the celery sticks into large pieces. Peel and slice the carrots thinly. Slice the cabbage, and top and tail the beans. Remove the seeds from the peppers and dice the flesh.

PREPARATION: 25 MINUTES
COOKING: 4-6 MINUTES
SERVES: 4-6

4 Heat the groundnut oil in a small wok or frying pan. Add the red curry paste and stir well over low heat for 1-2 minutes. Add the coconut cream, soy sauce, lime juice, sugar, salt, spices and peanuts. Stir well and heat through gently for 3-4 minutes. Pour over the vegetables and toss gently. Transfer to a serving dish and serve warm garnished with sprigs of mint.

FRIED MIXED VEGETABLES

Bhud bhug raum mid

125g/4oz cabbage

125g/4oz cauliflower

125g/4oz broccoli

2 carrots

125g/4oz mushrooms

1 onion

3 tablespoons vegetable oil

1 garlic clove, crushed

½ teaspoon freshly ground black pepper

2 tablespoons oyster sauce

150ml/¼ pint chicken or vegetable stock

50g/2oz bean sprouts

2 Heat the oil in a wok or deep frying pan. Add the crushed garlic and then stir-fry quickly over medium heat until golden. Do not allow it to get too brown.

3 Add the shredded cabbage and cauliflower florets, and a generous grinding of black pepper. Stir in the oyster sauce and the chicken or vegetable stock, and then cook, stirring constantly, for 3 minutes.

4 Add the broccoli, carrots, mushrooms and onion to the wok together with the bean sprouts. Stir-fry for 2 minutes. Transfer the fried vegetables to a large dish or platter and serve immediately.

1 Shred the cabbage and separate the cauliflower florets. Trim and slice the broccoli. Scrape the carrots and cut into matchstick strips. Wipe the mushrooms on some kitchen paper and slice thinly. Peel and slice the onion into rings.

PREPARATION: 15 MINUTES
COOKING: 6-7 MINUTES
SERVES: 4

AUBERGINE WITH SHRIMP PASTE SAUCE

Nam prig bhug

1 Make the shrimp paste sauce: put the chopped garlic and red chillies in a mortar and then grind them until they are well blended and form a thick paste.

3 Cut the aubergines into thick slices. Put the beaten egg in a shallow bowl and dip the aubergine slices into it until they are all well coated with egg.

2 Transfer the garlic and chilli paste to a small bowl and add the shrimp paste, lemon juice, sugar, nam pla and ground dried shrimp. Mix well together until they are thoroughly combined. Set aside while you cook the aubergines.

PREPARATION: 15 MINUTES
COOKING: 5-10 MINUTES
SERVES: 4

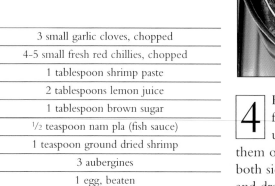

| 3 small garlic cloves, chopped |
| 4-5 small fresh red chillies, chopped |
| 1 tablespoon shrimp paste |
| 2 tablespoons lemon juice |
| 1 tablespoon brown sugar |
| ½ teaspoon nam pla (fish sauce) |
| 1 teaspoon ground dried shrimp |
| 3 aubergines |
| 1 egg, beaten |
| oil for deep frying |

4 Heat the oil for deep frying and fry the aubergine slices in batches until they are golden brown. Turn them once during cooking to brown both sides. Remove with a slotted spoon and drain on absorbent kitchen paper. Serve hot with the shrimp paste sauce.

STUFFED AUBERGINES

Kayanthi hnat

1 Wash the aubergines and pat dry. Cut off the tops and scoop out the centres. Cut the scooped-out flesh into small dice. Season with a little salt and set aside. Fill the scooped-out shells with salted water and stand for 3-4 minutes before emptying and rinsing the shells in fresh water.

24 small Thai aubergines
salt
50g/2oz uncooked prawns, peeled
75g/3oz chicken breast, skinned and boned
1 spring onion, finely chopped
4 garlic cloves, crushed
1 tablespoon chilli powder
1 teaspoon turmeric
1 tablespoon chopped fresh coriander or parsley
2 tablespoons vegetable oil
1 egg
3 tablespoons cornflour
3 tablespoons plain flour
oil for deep frying
To serve:
chilli sauce (see page 110)

2 Chop the prawns and chicken into small dice and place in a bowl. Add the spring onion, garlic and diced aubergine, and mix well. Season with chilli powder, turmeric and chopped coriander or parsley. Bind the ingredients together with the vegetable oil, and season with extra salt. Knead to a smooth paste and use this mixture to fill the aubergines.

3 Make a thick batter: mix together the egg, cornflour and flour in a bowl, and add a little salt and cold water. Beat until smooth. Dip the filled aubergines into the batter so that they are thoroughly coated.

4 Heat the oil for deep frying in a wok, large saucepan or deep-fat fryer, and fry the aubergines, a few at a time, until crisp and golden brown all over. Remove with a slotted spoon and drain on absorbent kitchen paper. Serve with chilli sauce.

PREPARATION: 30 MINUTES
COOKING: 7-10 MINUTES
SERVES: 4-6

STICKY RICE WITH MANGOES

Mamuang kuo nieo

1 Soak the glutinous rice in cold water overnight. The following day, drain the rice and put it with the coconut milk, sugar and salt in a large saucepan. Bring slowly to the boil, then reduce the heat and simmer gently until all the coconut milk has been absorbed by the rice. Stir the mixture occasionally.

3 Peel the mangoes and slice off the succulent yellow flesh by standing the mangoes upright and cutting down on either side of the stone. Cut the flesh into thin slices or 'fans' with a sharp knife.

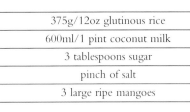

2 Put the cooked rice in the top of a foil-lined steamer, and steam gently for 15-20 minutes over simmering water. Press the rice into an oiled baking tray, spreading it out flat and pressing down hard. Set aside until it is firm and thoroughly cooled. Cut the rice into slices or diamond shapes.

| 375g/12oz glutinous rice |
| 600ml/1 pint coconut milk |
| 3 tablespoons sugar |
| pinch of salt |
| 3 large ripe mangoes |
| **To serve:** |
| 3 tablespoons palm or brown sugar |
| 3 tablespoons water |

PREPARATION: 20 MINUTES
COOKING: 35-40 MINUTES
SERVES: 6

4 Put the palm or brown sugar in a small saucepan with the water. Heat gently over low heat, stirring all the time until the sugar is completely dissolved. Serve the rice slices or diamonds with the mango slices. Pour over a little of the sugar syrup.

103

COCONUT PANCAKES

Khan um kluk

600ml/1 pint coconut milk

100g/3½oz rice flour

3 eggs

125g/4oz sugar

100g/3½oz desiccated coconut

pink and green food colouring

salt

oil for frying

To serve:

grated coconut

1 Make the batter: put the coconut milk, rice flour, eggs and sugar in a large bowl and beat for 5 minutes. Fold the desiccated coconut into the batter.

2 Divide the batter into 3 equal portions in 3 bowls. Colour one pink, one green and leave the other plain. Add a pinch of salt to each bowl and beat well. Leave to stand for at least 20 minutes.

3 Wipe a 15cm/6 inch omelette pan with an oiled cloth and heat gently. When hot, pour in a thin layer of batter and, tilting the pan, swirl it around to cover the base thinly. Cook over moderate heat until set and flecked with brown underneath. Flip over and cook the other side. Roll up and slide on to a plate.

4 Cook the remaining pancakes in the same way and keep warm. Stack the different colours in groups on a serving plate. Serve warm, scattered with grated coconut, with some fresh fruit.

PREPARATION: 15 MINUTES +
20 MINUTES STANDING TIME
COOKING: 15 MINUTES
SERVES: 6-8

FRIED COCONUT CAKES

Mok si kao

1 Put the sugar and water in a saucepan and heat gently, stirring all the time until the sugar dissolves. Bring to the boil, and then cook gently for 2-3 minutes until slightly reduced and syrupy. Remove from the heat and set aside to cool.

2 Put the rice flour, egg, baking powder, salt and coconut in a large mixing bowl. Mix all the ingredients together to a smooth paste.

PREPARATION: 20 MINUTES +
20 MINUTES STANDING
COOKING: 5-10 MINUTES
SERVES: 4

3 Pour in the cooled syrup and beat to make a smooth batter. Set aside for 20 minutes. Core the apples and cut into rings, and peel and slice the bananas. Add the fruit to the batter.

100g/3½oz palm sugar or brown sugar
450ml/¾ pint water
300g/10oz rice flour
1 egg
2 teaspoons baking powder
pinch of salt
125g/4oz grated fresh or desiccated coconut
2 apples
2 bananas
oil for deep frying

4 Heat the oil in a heavy saucepan, wok or deep-fat fryer, and drop in some large spoonfuls of the fruit batter. Fry in batches until golden brown on both sides, turning once. Remove and drain on absorbent kitchen paper. Serve hot with fresh fruit.

STICKY RICE WITH COCONUT MILK

Khow-nheaw moon

1 Wash the glutinous rice, cover with water and soak for at least 3 hours. Drain thoroughly and spread it out in the top of a large steamer. Place over boiling water and steam for 30-40 minutes.

2 Make the custard: combine all the ingredients in a mixing bowl and beat well with a hand-held whisk. Divide between 6-8 small basins or moulds(or 4 coconut shells) and place in the top of one or two steamers.

PREPARATION: 40-50 MINUTES +
3 HOURS SOAKING
COOKING: 30 MINUTES
SERVES: 6

3 Place over boiling water and steam for 30 minutes, taking care that the water underneath does not boil dry. To test whether they are cooked, insert the point of a sharp knife into one of the custards – it should come out clean if they are cooked.

500g/1lb glutinous rice	
400ml/14 fl oz coconut milk	
175g/6oz sugar	
1 tablespoon salt	
For the custard:	
6 eggs	
250ml/8 fl oz coconut milk	
175g/6oz demerara sugar	
125g/4oz caster sugar	
1 teaspoon vanilla essence	
To serve:	
sliced mango	

4 While the custards are cooking, combine the coconut milk, sugar and salt in a saucepan and bring to the boil over moderate heat, stirring constantly. When it boils, stir in the cooked rice, remove from the heat and cover the pan. Leave to stand for 15 minutes. Serve with the turned-out custards and sliced mango.

SAUCES AND CURRY PASTES

CHILLI SAUCE
Nam jeem

8 fresh red chillies, chopped
4 garlic cloves, crushed
1 tablespoon nam pla (fish sauce)
2 teaspoons sugar
juice of 1 lime or lemon
1/4 teaspoon salt
125ml/4 fl oz water
2 tablespoons groundnut oil

Put the chillies, garlic, nam pla, sugar, lime or lemon juice and the salt in a small saucepan. Stir in the water and oil. Bring to the boil, reduce the heat and simmer gently for 10-15 minutes. Blend until smooth in a food processor or blender. Store in a screwtop jar in the refrigerator for a maximum of 2 weeks. Use as required.

SHRIMP DIPPING SAUCE
Kapee khua

3 dried red chillies, seeded and soaked in boiling water until soft
2 tablespoons chopped lemon grass
6 shallots, finely chopped
3 tablespoons shrimp paste
50g/2oz dried shrimp
300ml/1/2 pint coconut milk
125g/4oz minced pork
4 fresh red chillies
3 tablespoons palm or demerara sugar
3 tablespoons nam pla (fish sauce)

Grind the soaked red chillies, lemon grass, shallots and shrimp paste in a blender, food processor or mortar. Add the dried shrimp and grind to a smooth paste. Bring the coconut milk to the boil in a saucepan, lower the heat and simmer for 10 minutes. Add the ground chilli paste and cook, stirring constantly, for 5 minutes. Add the minced pork and whole chillies, and cook, stirring, for 10 minutes. Stir in the sugar and nam pla. Serve with fried fish, prawns or vegetables.

THAI HOT SAUCE
Nam prik

2 tablespoons dried shrimps, soaked
3 teaspoons salt
1 teaspoon brown sugar
4 garlic cloves
6 anchovy fillets or 1 tablespoon salted anchovy essence
1 tablespoon soya sauce
4 fresh red chillies
lime juice

Put all the ingredients, except the lime juice, in a mortar and pound with a pestle to a smooth paste. Alternatively, whizz in a food processor or blender. Sprinkle with lime juice to taste and stir into the sauce. Store in a screwtop jar for up to 2 weeks. Serve with meat, vegetables, noodles and rice dishes.

PLUM SAUCE
Num beuy

3 preserved plums plus 1 tablespoon liquid from the jar
150ml/1/4 pint water
6 tablespoons caster sugar

Put the plums, the plum liquid and water in a saucepan and mix well together. Bring to the boil, and allow to boil for 1-2 minutes, stirring constantly with a wooden spoon to break up the plums. Press the mixture through a sieve and strain into the pan. Add the sugar, stirring well until dissolved, and bring back to the boil. Reduce the heat and simmer for 15 minutes, or until the sauce thickens and turns reddish in colour. When cool, pour into a screwtop jar and store in the refrigerator.

GARLIC MIXTURE
Kra tium-prig tai

2 tablespoons crushed garlic
2 tablespoons chopped coriander root or stem
1/2 tablespoon ground black pepper

This simple garlic mixture is a fundamental ingredient in Thai cooking and appears in many of the recipes in this book. Pound all the ingredients together in a mortar with a pestle until they are thoroughly blended and form a paste. If wished, it can be made in advance and stored, covered, in the refrigerator for 1-2 days until required. This will enhance the flavour.

GARLIC OIL
Num mun kra tium

4 tablespoons vegetable or sunflower oil
1 tablespoon crushed garlic

Heat the oil in a small frying pan and then add the crushed garlic. Cook slowly over gentle heat until the garlic is golden, stirring occasionally. Use in recipes as required.

RED CURRY PASTE
Kang bhed dang

6 dried red chillies
2 tablespoons chopped lemon grass
1 tablespoon chopped coriander root or stem
1 tablespoon chopped shallot
1 tablespoon chopped garlic
1 teaspoon chopped galanga(khar root)
2 teaspoons coriander seeds
1 teaspoon cumin seeds
6 white peppercorns
1 teaspoon salt
1 teaspoon shrimp paste

Scoop the seeds out of the chillies, and then soak them in cold water for 10 minutes. Drain well and chop roughly. Put the chopped chillies in a blender or food processor and add the remaining ingredients. Process to a smooth paste. Alternatively, you can pound the mixture in a large mortar with a pestle. Store in a screwtop jar in the refrigerator for up to 3 weeks. Use as required.

GREEN CURRY PASTE

6 dried green chillies
3 tablespoons chopped spring onions
1 tablespoon chopped garlic
1 tablespoon powdered lemon grass
1 tablespoon shrimp paste
1 teaspoon ground laos
1 teaspoon caraway seeds
2 teaspoons coriander seeds
1 teaspoon finely grated lemon rind
1 teaspoon salt

Wash the chillies under running cold water. Remove the stems and brush out any seeds. Put the chillies in a blender or food processor with the remaining ingredients and blend at high speed for 20-30 seconds, or until the mixture is a smooth paste. Alternatively, pound the mixture in a mortar with a pestle. Store in a small screwtop jar in the refrigerator for up to 3 weeks. Use as required.

COCONUT CREAM & MILK
Kati gon

400g/14oz grated or desiccated coconut
900ml/1½ pints milk

Mix the coconut and milk together in a saucepan. Bring to the boil, and then lower the heat and simmer, stirring occasionally, until the mixture is reduced by one-third. Strain, pressing the mixture against the sides of the strainer to extract as much liquid as possible. Pour the strained coconut milk into a bowl and chill in the refrigerator. When it is really cold, skim off the thicker 'cream' that rises to the surface. The remaining liquid is the coconut milk.

TAMARIND WATER
Num som ma kharm

25g/1oz tamarind
150ml/¼ pint warm water

Wash the tamarind and leave it to soak in the warm water for 5-10 minutes; the longer you leave it to soak, the stronger the flavour. Squeeze out as much tamarind pulp as possible, and then press the thickened liquid through a sieve. Use immediately. If you wish to store the tamarind juice, you must strain it into a saucepan and bring to the boil. Remove from the heat and allow to cool in the pan before transferring the juice to a bowl. Cover and store in the refrigerator.

INDEX

A

Aubergine(s),
    with shrimp paste sauce, 98-99
    stuffed, 100-101

B

Beef,
    with cashew nuts, 46-47
    curry, thick red, 58-59
    masaman curry, 54-55
    in oyster sauce, 56-57
    salad, north-eastern, 90-91
    sauce, rice sticks with, 78-79

C

Chicken,
    and coconut soup, 12-13
    curry, 62-63
    dumplings, 24-25
    ginger, with honey, 66-67
    salad, 92-93
    wings, stuffed, 64-65
Chilli sauce, 110
Coconut,
    cakes, fried, 106-107
    cream, 111
    milk, 111
    pancakes, 104-105
Crab in the shell, 32-33
Crispy rice,
    with dipping sauce, 72-73
    vermicelli, 86-87
Curried vegetable salad, 94-95
Curry(ies),
    chicken, 62-63
    masaman, 54-55
    paste, green, 111
        red, 111
    prawn, 30-31
    sour fish, 34-35
    thick red beef, 58-59

D

Desserts,
    coconut pancakes, 104-105
    fried coconut cakes, 106-107

sticky rice, with coconut
    milk, 108-109
    with mangoes, 102-103
Dumplings,
    chicken, 24-25
    Thai, 22-23

E

Egg(s),
    -fried noodles, 84-85
    Thai hard-boiled, 88-89

F

Fish,
    balls, fried hot, 28-29
    cakes, spicy, 44-45
    curry, sour, 34-35
    steamed, 42-43
Fried coconut pancakes, 106-107
Fried golden bags, 26-27
Fried hot fish balls, 28-29
Fried mixed vegetables, 96-97
Fried noodles with vegetables,
    82-83
Fried pork balls, 60-61
Fried rice with pork, 74-75
Fried wonton, 16-17

G

Garlic mixture, 110
Garlic oil, 111
Ginger chicken with honey,
    66-67
Green curry paste, 111

M

Mangoes, sticky rice with,
    102-103
Masaman curry, 54-55
Mussels with Thai herbs, 38-39

N

Noodles,
    -egg-fried, 84-85
    fried, with vegetables, 82-83
North-eastern beef salad, 90-91

O

Oyster sauce, beef in, 56-57

P

Pancake, stuffed Thai, 52-53
Plum sauce, 110-111
Pork,
    balls, fried, 60-61
    fried rice with, 74-75
    with hot sauces, sliced, 50-51
    on skewers, 18-19
    sweet and sour, 48-49
Prawn(s),
    in coconut sauce, 40-41
    curry, 30-31
    and squid hot soup, 14-15

R

Red curry paste, 111
Rice,
    crispy, with dipping auce,
        72-73
    fried, with pork, 74-75
    spicy fried, 80-81
    sticks, with beef sauce, 78-79
        Thai-style fried, 76-77
    sticky, with coconut milk,
        108-109
        with mangoes, 102-103
    vermicelli, crispy, 86-87
        in coconut milk, 70-71
        with sauce, 68-69

S

Salad(s),
    chicken, 92-93
    curried vegetable, 94-95
    north-eastern beef, 90-91
Satay, 18-19
Sauce(s),
    chilli, 110
    hot, 50
    plum, 110
    shrimp dipping, 110
    shrimp paste, 98
    Thai hot, 110

Seafood in batter, 36-37
Shrimp dipping sauce, 110
Shrimp paste sauce, aubergine
    with, 98-99
Shrimp soup, 10-11
Sliced pork with hot sauces,
    50-51
Soup(s),
    chicken and coconut, 12-13
    prawn and squid hot, 14-15
    shrimp, 10-11
Sour fish curry, 34-35
Spicy fishcakes, 44-45
Spicy fried rice, 80-81
Spring rolls, 20-21
Steamed fish, 42-43
Sticky rice,
    with coconut milk, 108-109
    with mangoes, 102-103
Stuffed aubergines, 100-101
Stuffed chicken wings, 64-65
Stuffed Thai pancake, 52-53
Sweet and sour pork, 48-49

T

Tamarind water, 111
Tang tong, 26-27
Thai dumplings, 22-23
Thai hard-boiled eggs, 88-89
Thai hot sauce, 110-111
Thai-style fried rice sticks, 76-77
Thick red beef curry, 58-59

V

Vegetable(s),
    aubergine with shrimp paste
        sauce, 98-99
    fried mixed, 96-97
    fried noodles with, 82-83
    salad, curried, 94-95
    stuffed aubergines, 100-101
Vermicelli,
    crispy rice, 86-87
    rice, in coconut milk, 70-71
    rice, with sauce, 68-69
Wonton, fried, 16-17